THIS B...
BELO...

Name: Age:

Favourite player:

2023/24

My Predictions   **Actual**

The Foxes' final position:

The Foxes' top scorer:

EFL Championship winners:

EFL Championship top scorer:

FA Cup winners:

EFL Cup winners:

Contributors: Peter Rogers

A TWOCAN PUBLICATION

©2023. Published by twocan under licence from LEICESTER CITY Football Club.

Every effort has been made to ensure the accuracy of information within this publication but the publishers cannot be held responsible for any errors or omissions. Views expressed are those of the authors and do not necessarily represent those of the publishers or the football club. All rights reserved.

978-1-915571-59-5

PICTURE CREDITS: Action Images, Alamy, Leicester City Football Club, Press Association

CONTENTS

EFL Championship Squad 2023/24	6
Soccer Skills: Shooting From Distance	22
Kiernan Dewsbury-Hall Poster	23
LCFC Women	24
Dazzling Defenders	26
Kelechi Iheanacho Poster	28
Footy Phrases Wordsearch	29
Players Of The Season	30
Soccer Skills: The Wall Pass	32
Cesare Casadei Poster	33
A-Z Quiz	34
Jamie Vardy Poster	38
Design A Footy Boot	39
Midfield Maestros	40
Classic Fan'tastic	42
James Justin Poster	44
Callum Doyle Poster	45
Goals Of The Season	46
Behind The Badge	48
Harry Winks Poster	50
True Colours	51
Formidable Forwards	52
Rewind - Fast Forward	54
Soccer Skills: Turning With The Ball	56
Stephy Mavididi Poster	57
High Fives Quiz	58
Sensational Stoppers	60
Answers	62

EFL CHAMPIONSHIP SQUAD 2023/24

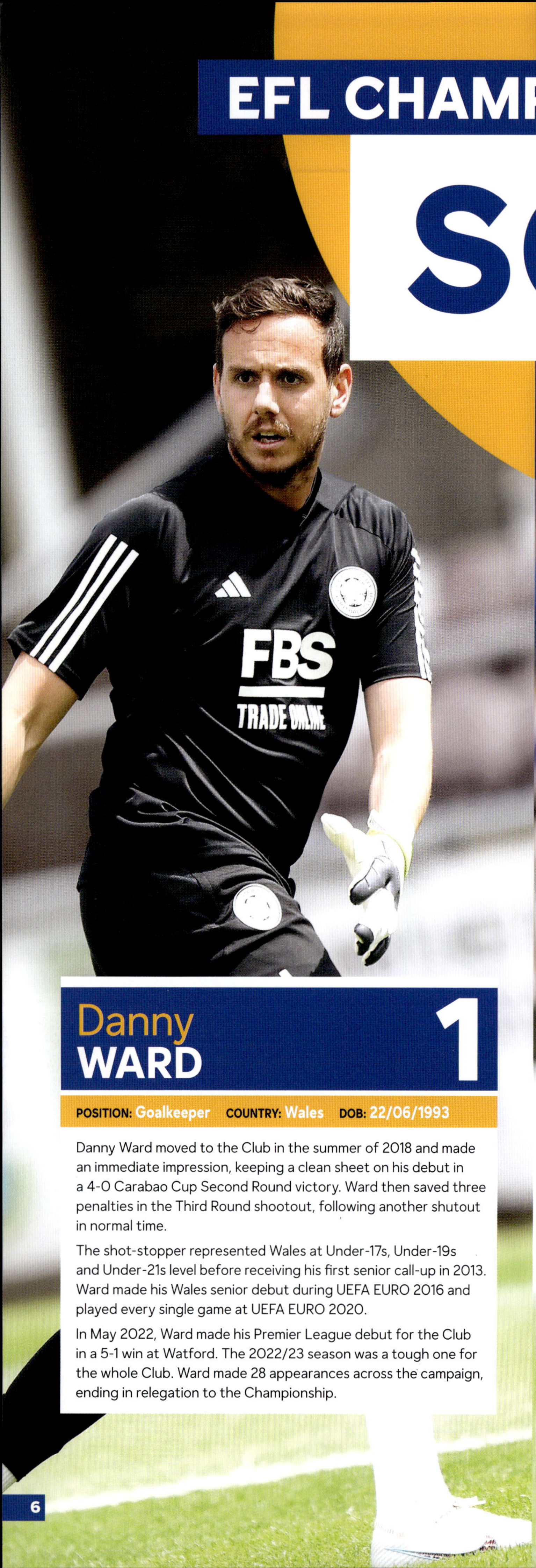

Danny WARD — 1

POSITION: Goalkeeper **COUNTRY:** Wales **DOB:** 22/06/1993

Danny Ward moved to the Club in the summer of 2018 and made an immediate impression, keeping a clean sheet on his debut in a 4-0 Carabao Cup Second Round victory. Ward then saved three penalties in the Third Round shootout, following another shutout in normal time.

The shot-stopper represented Wales at Under-17s, Under-19s and Under-21s level before receiving his first senior call-up in 2013. Ward made his Wales senior debut during UEFA EURO 2016 and played every single game at UEFA EURO 2020.

In May 2022, Ward made his Premier League debut for the Club in a 5-1 win at Watford. The 2022/23 season was a tough one for the whole Club. Ward made 28 appearances across the campaign, ending in relegation to the Championship.

James JUSTIN — 2

POSITION: Defender **COUNTRY:** England **DOB:** 23/02/1998

The full-back, who can play on either defensive flank, marked his Foxes debut with a goal in a 4-0 Carabao Cup Second Round victory away at his former club, Luton Town, in September 2019. In 2020/21, Justin became an invaluable figure for the Foxes, making 31 appearances in all competitions, until an ACL injury cruelly cut short a promising season for the former England Under-21s international.

In the summer of 2022, a reward for his talents and his determined recovery from serious injury, arrived in the form of a first-ever call-up to Gareth Southgate's England squad ahead of four UEFA Nations League fixtures in June. He made his debut, from the start, in a UEFA Nations League group stage clash away at Hungary.

Wout FAES — 3

POSITION: Defender   **COUNTRY:** Belgium   **DOB:** 03/04/1998

Faes emerged through the youth academy at Belgium giants Anderlecht from the age of 14, following in the footsteps of some of the country's greatest defenders. Faes' leadership skills came to the fore as he captained Anderlecht's Academy, and after two successful loan spells in Holland at the beginning of his senior career, were recognised at Belgian first-tier club Oostende too.

The defender made the switch to Reims and built upon a successful first season by becoming a leading Ligue 1 player during the 2021/22 campaign. Now entering the latest phase of his developing career, following his switch to England, the Belgian has become a favourite with his dedicated and impressive displays in defence.

Conor COADY — 4

POSITION: Defender   **COUNTRY:** England   **DOB:** 25/02/1993

Continuing to be named in national team squads, including the 2020 UEFA European Championship that England finished as runners-up, Coady is renowned as a commanding presence at the back.

A product of Liverpool's esteemed youth academy, Coady enjoyed fruitful spells at Sheffield United and Huddersfield Town before Wolves became his next destination. The anchor in a three-man central defensive partnership, Coady was an ever-present in the side across multiple seasons, earning a spot in the EFL Championship Team of the Season, the EFL Team of the Season and UEFA's 2019/20 Europa League Squad of the Season.

The 6ft 1in centre-half can also prove a threat in the opposition box, demonstrated on the international stage when he scored against Wales at Wembley. With a further 24 league appearances under his belt on loan at Everton last term, the 30-year-old entered the 2023/24 Championship season as one of the most experienced figures in the Foxes' squad.

Callum DOYLE 5

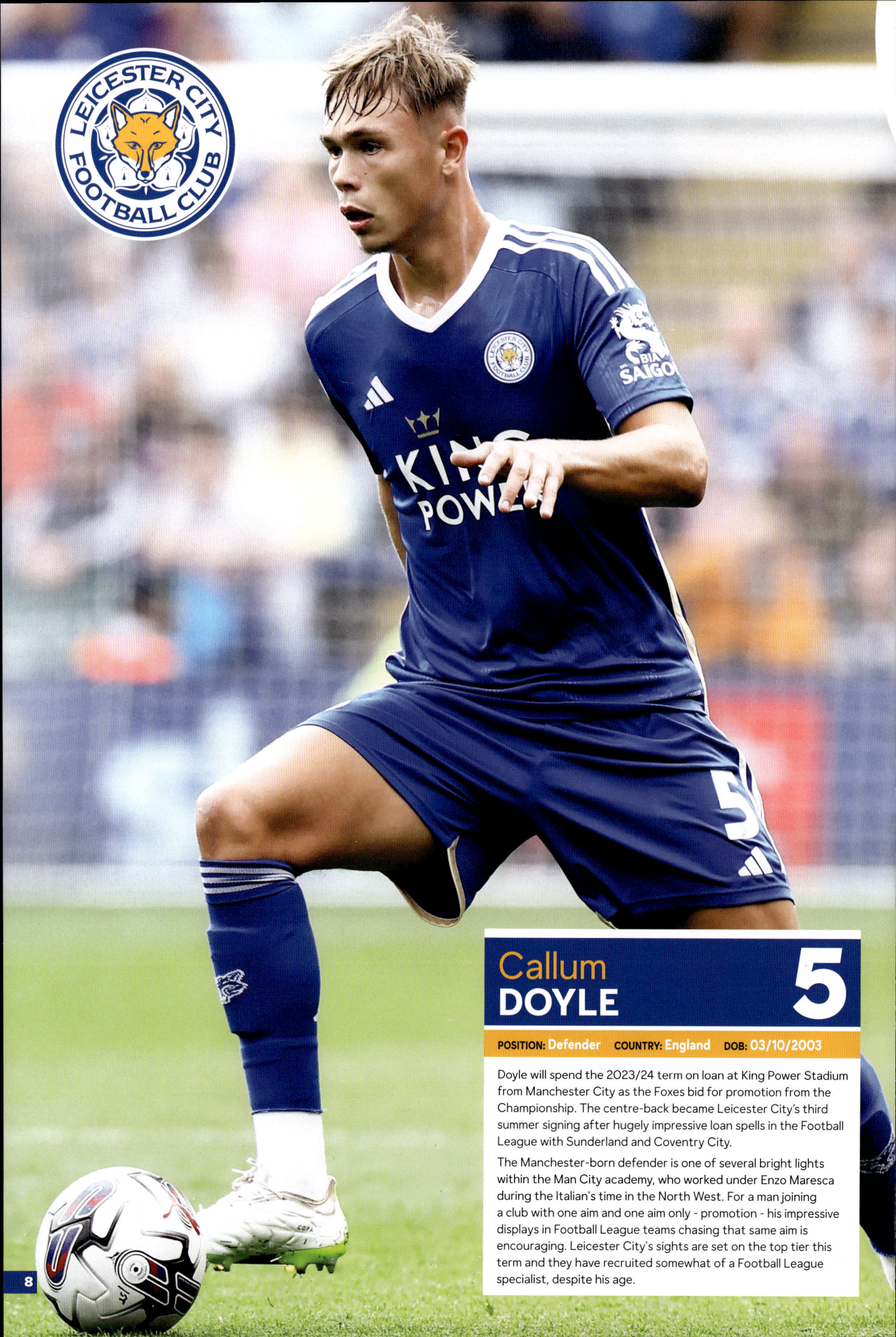

POSITION: Defender **COUNTRY:** England **DOB:** 03/10/2003

Doyle will spend the 2023/24 term on loan at King Power Stadium from Manchester City as the Foxes bid for promotion from the Championship. The centre-back became Leicester City's third summer signing after hugely impressive loan spells in the Football League with Sunderland and Coventry City.

The Manchester-born defender is one of several bright lights within the Man City academy, who worked under Enzo Maresca during the Italian's time in the North West. For a man joining a club with one aim and one aim only - promotion - his impressive displays in Football League teams chasing that same aim is encouraging. Leicester City's sights are set on the top tier this term and they have recruited somewhat of a Football League specialist, despite his age.

EFL CHAMPIONSHIP
SQUAD
2023/24

Cesare CASADEI — 7

POSITION: Midfielder **COUNTRY:** Italy **DOB:** 10/01/2003

Born in Ravenna, Italy, the central midfielder began his career with Inter Milan, spending four years progressing through the Nerazzurri's youth system before joining Chelsea in August 2022.

An Italian youth international, the playmaker was a key member of the Italy Under-20 side that reached the final of the FIFA U20 World Cup in Argentina, with his performances earning him the Golden Ball and the Golden Boot awards. Casadei has represented Italy at various youth levels, from the Under-16s to the Under-21s, playing more than 30 times for his nation.

The talented 20-year-old also has previous loan experience in the Championship with Reading last term. His life at King Power Stadium could hardly have got off to a better start - a 92nd-minute winner against Cardiff City on his debut.

Harry WINKS — 8

POSITION: Midfielder **COUNTRY:** England **DOB:** 02/02/1996

Growing up a Tottenham fan, having been born and raised on the outskirts of north London, Winks joined his boyhood club at the age of five. A 20-year long association with Spurs would culminate with a starting appearance in the Club's first-ever Champions League Final, though it would end in defeat.

Impressive performances resulted Winks being brought into the international fold by England for the UEFA Nations League, with his maiden senior England goal following during EURO 2020 qualifying. The cultured central midfielder also spent time in Italy last term, furthering his experience with a loan spell at Sampdoria.

With more than a century of Premier League appearances under his belt, Leicester have acquired an accomplished English midfielder. A talented passer, possessing an ability to play as a deep-lying playmaker, the 27-year-old's qualities are sure to come to the fore again this season.

EFL CHAMPIONSHIP SQUAD 2023/24

Jamie VARDY — 9

POSITION: Forward **COUNTRY:** England **DOB:** 11/01/1987

Jamie Vardy's rise from non-league to Premier League champion and FA Cup winner - also representing England at a FIFA World Cup, joining the Premier League 100 Club and winning the Golden Boot – is one of the most inspirational fables in modern times.

Since joining the Foxes in 2012, Vardy has become one of the most famous footballers on the planet and was a major protagonist of City's stunning 2016 Premier League title victory. He is now the Club's third top goalscorer of all time, behind Arthur Chandler and Arthur Rowley.

As well as rising to the status of England international, the pacy striker has consistently hit double figures in the majority of his seasons spent as a Fox and is the Club's all-time highest Premier League goalscorer. In total, he has earned 26 caps for England, scoring seven goals. With so many iconic, memorable and simply stunning strikes among them, Vardy's overall LCFC tally in all competitions currently stands at over 150 goals.

Stephy MAVIDIDI — 10

POSITION: Forward **COUNTRY:** England **DOB:** 31/05/1998

City added attacking talent Stephy Mavididi to the Club's ranks in the summer of 2023 from French Ligue 1 side Montpellier. The 25-year-old signed a five-year deal with the Football Club.

Having enjoyed four seasons in the top flight of French football, he built a reputation as an exciting and versatile forward. The former England youth international also became the most-capped English player in Ligue 1 history during 2022/23 when he overtook Chris Waddle's record by making a 108th appearance in the division.

The Derby-born attacker also boasts EFL experience having previously represented Charlton Athletic and Preston North End in League 1 and the Championship, respectively, during loan spells in the early stages of his career. City supporters will be hoping that Mavididi can build upon his impressive start to the 2023/24 season under Enzo Maresca.

Marc ALBRIGHTON 11

POSITION: Midfielder   **COUNTRY:** England   **DOB:** 18/11/1989

Marc Albrighton has spent nine successful years as a Leicester City player since ending a long association with Aston Villa in 2014, winning the Premier League, the Emirates FA Cup and the FA Community Shield with the Foxes.

City's No.11 has also represented the Club in the UEFA Champions League, UEFA Europa League and the UEFA Europa Conference League, making over 280 appearances for the Foxes in that time.

At the start of the 2022/23 campaign, Albrighton became City's vice-captain. Returning from a brief loan spell at West Bromwich Albion, the experienced winger will be an influential figure in the dressing room as the Foxes aim to gain promotion back to the Premier League.

Alex SMITHIES 12

POSITION: Goalkeeper   **COUNTRY:** England   **DOB:** 05/03/1990

Alex Smithies, a seasoned professional with previous Championship experience, joined the Foxes on a two-year deal in 2022. He started his career with Huddersfield Town, where he spent eight seasons, making over 200 appearances for the Terriers.

A switch to Queens Park Rangers followed in 2015 for Smithies, spending three years at Loftus Road before moving to South Wales in 2018. While at Cardiff, the shot-stopper established himself as an important figure, playing a total of 100 times for the Bluebirds in all competitions.

Kelechi IHEANACHO — 14

POSITION: Forward **COUNTRY:** Nigeria **DOB:** 03/10/1996

Nigeria international Kelechi Iheanacho has been an effective attacking option for the Foxes, netting over 50 goals since signing from Manchester City in 2017. Early in his career at the Club the forward made English football history, becoming the first player to have scored a goal awarded by VAR (Video Assistant Referee).

In 2020/21, he netted his first hat-trick for the Club in a 5-0 win over Sheffield United. The campaign ended with 19 goals in all competitions for the Nigerian, who helped the Foxes finally lift the Emirates FA Cup for the first time, in a season which ended with Iheanacho winning the Club's Goal of the Season prize for a spectacular effort against Crystal Palace.

In early 2023, Iheanacho made another impact upon returning to the XI, scoring in three successive games, helping City to wins over Walsall (FA Cup), Aston Villa and Tottenham Hotspur.

Harry SOUTTAR — 15

POSITION: Defender **COUNTRY:** Australia **DOB:** 22/10/1998

Australia international Harry Souttar signed for Leicester City in January 2023 - adding defensive steel to the Club's options at the back. A key part of the Socceroos side which equalled their best-ever FIFA World Cup display last year, Souttar's stock has been rising quickly over recent years.

Standing at a giant 6ft 6ins, there's nobody taller in City's senior squad than the Club's new centre-back. Souttar's debut came at Aston Villa in early February and earned plaudits for his overall display. He continued to feature in the side regularly until the end of the campaign.

EFL CHAMPIONSHIP SQUAD 2023/24

Hamza CHOUDHURY — 17

POSITION: Midfielder **COUNTRY:** England **DOB:** 01/10/1997

Midfielder Hamza Choudhury has been at Leicester City since 2005, going on to make over 80 appearances for the Foxes, including their triumphant appearance in the final of the Emirates FA Cup in 2021.

Choudhury joined the Club's Academy at the age of just seven and, as well as climbing through the ranks, was regularly a ball boy at King Power Stadium. Now, the tough-tackling midfielder is a first-team player and an England Under-21s international.

After spending the previous campaign on loan at Watford in the Championship, Choudhury committed his future to the Club by signing a new contract on his return.

Abdul FATAWU — 18

POSITION: Forward **COUNTRY:** Ghana **DOB:** 08/03/2004

Born in the northern city of Tamale in Ghana in 2004, Abdul Fatawu became Leicester City's eighth summer signing in late August 2023. The attacking midfielder joined the Club on a season-long loan, hoping to add firepower to Enzo Maresca's promotion charge at King Power Stadium.

Fatawu's career is already in full swing despite being just 19 - he's a full international, capped 14 times for Ghana, including at a FIFA World Cup, while also playing in the UEFA Champions League with Sporting Lisbon. Helping Leicester City return to the Premier League is his next assignment.

EFL CHAMPIONSHIP SQUAD 2023/24

Patson DAKA — 20

POSITION: Forward **COUNTRY:** Zambia **DOB:** 09/10/1998

At the age of just 16 in 2015, Daka was called up to Zambia's senior squad to make the first of more than 30 appearances for his country. On 1 July 2021, a move to the Foxes was confirmed as Patson prepared for his maiden campaign in the Premier League.

His first goal arrived in Leicester's 4-2 win over Manchester United at King Power Stadium. Shortly after, Daka made headlines across the continent as he became the first Foxes player since 1958 to score four goals in a single fixture as he netted all the goals in a stunning 4-3 comeback success over Spartak Moscow in the UEFA Europa League.

Into the New Year, goals against Tottenham Hotspur, Brighton & Hove Albion, Randers and Everton took his tally to 11 in his first season in Leicester. The pacey forward went on to make 36 appearances in all competitions during 2022/23, contributing four goals towards the Club's unsuccessful attempt to retain Premier League status.

Ricardo PEREIRA — 21

POSITION: Defender **COUNTRY:** Portugal **DOB:** 06/10/1993

Over Ricardo's time at the Club to date, since signing from FC Porto, the Portugal international has represented his country at the FIFA World Cup and built a reputation as one of the most talented players at an elite level.

Notable moments include his stunning winner against Manchester City in December 2018, while also netting in the Club's highest-ever home top-flight win, a 5-0 rout of Newcastle United in September 2019. In 2022, meanwhile, he also struck the winner in City's quarter-final tie against PSV Eindhoven in the UEFA Europa Conference League.

Despite an ACL injury leading to a lengthy spell on the sidelines, featuring on 11 occasions in 2022/23, the Portuguese is now back for the Foxes and delivering typically impressive performances.

Kiernan DEWSBURY-HALL 22

POSITION: Midfielder **COUNTRY:** England **DOB:** 06/09/1998

After joining the Club aged eight, City's No.22 is now regarded as an integral member of the first-team squad, making 44 appearances in 2021/22, lifting the FA Community Shield, scoring three goals, and helping the side to reach the semi-final of the UEFA Europa Conference League. It was a campaign which also ended with a brace of individual awards as Dewsbury-Hall scooped Leicester's Players' Player and Young Player of the Season.

With the sound of his name being sung to the tune of Oasis' Wonderwall, Dewsbury-Hall has continued to impress, providing two goals and assists in 34 appearances in the 2022/23 season, despite the Club's eventual relegation. In June of that year, Dewsbury-Hall committed his future to the Club with a new deal until 2027. A player with real quality and tenacity, there is much excitement about what the future has in store for City's No.22.

Jannik VESTERGAARD 23

POSITION: Defender **COUNTRY:** Denmark **DOB:** 03/08/1992

The towering 6ft 6ins centre-back grew up in Denmark, where he spent time at several clubs as a youngster including Brøndby. After laying the foundations in his home nation, it was over in Germany where Vestergaard's footballing success for both club and country truly took off. Impressive performances for Hoffeinheim lead to Jannik being recognised as one of Denmark's best young talents, with his full senior international debut being made against Poland in 2014.

After showing consistency at the heart of defence for Werder Bremen and Borussia Mönchengladbach, Jannik developed his reputation as a gifted central defender in England's top-flight for Southampton. Despite not featuring often since signing for City in 2021, Vestergaard has started in multiple games under Enzo Maresca in the Championship this season.

EFL CHAMPIONSHIP SQUAD 2023/24

Wilfred NDIDI — 25

POSITION: Midfielder **COUNTRY:** Nigeria **DOB:** 16/12/1996

A midfielder with plenty of quality, Ndidi joined Leicester City from KRC Genk in January 2017 and eventually won the Emirates FA Cup with the Club in 2021. His time in Leicester is defined by his tremendous tackling ability, regularly seeing him feature at the top of the Premier League stats charts in previous years, while he has also starred in the UEFA Champions League, UEFA Europa League and the UEFA Europa Conference League.

Originally spotted playing for Nathaniel Boys in an open trial in the Nigerian city of Lagos, he started out as a central defender, before adapting superbly to a new defensive midfield role later in his career. In his first full season, Ndidi was the Premier League's top tackler after making 138 dispossessions, finishing ahead of former Fox N'Golo Kanté.

Despite injuries curtailing him briefly in recent seasons, the midfielder went on to make 30 appearances for City during the 2022/23 season.

Dennis PRAET — 26

POSITION: Midfielder **COUNTRY:** Belgium **DOB:** 14/05/1994

Belgium international Dennis Praet joined the Foxes from Sampdoria in 2019, since then he has taken his Foxes appearance tally beyond the half-century mark, scoring for the Club in the UEFA Europa League, and playing a role in Leicester's run to the final of the Emirates FA Cup in 2020/21.

The aspiring attacking midfielder's early years were spent at Den Dreef, the home of OHL, where his raw talent and tenacious personality shone through. In 2021/22, meanwhile, Praet spent a year on loan from Leicester City at Italian outfit Torino, making 24 appearances and netting two goals. The tenacious midfielder returned to the Club in the 2022/23 season, appearing on 27 occasions in all competitions.

EFL CHAMPIONSHIP SQUAD 2023/24

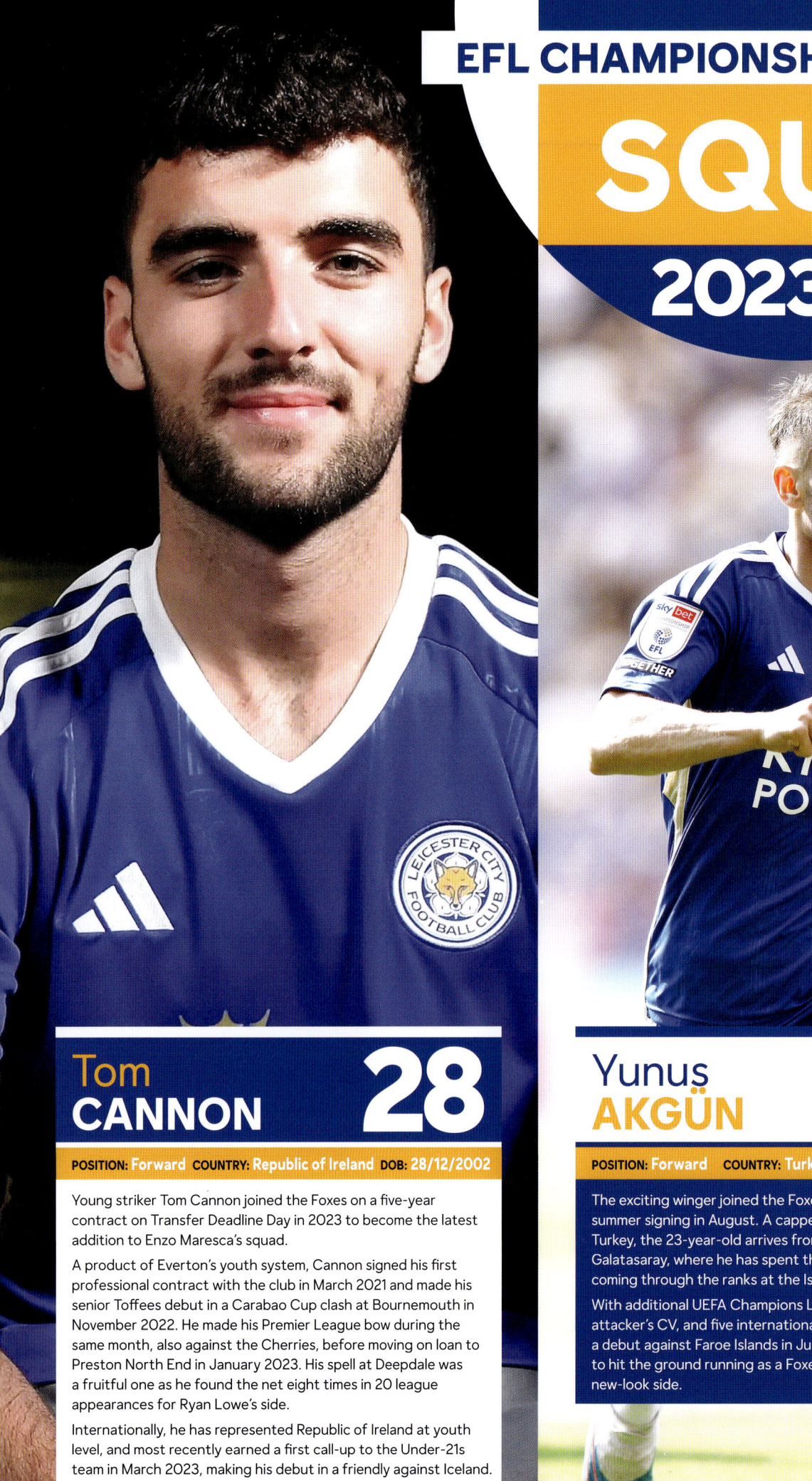

Tom CANNON — 28

POSITION: Forward **COUNTRY:** Republic of Ireland **DOB:** 28/12/2002

Young striker Tom Cannon joined the Foxes on a five-year contract on Transfer Deadline Day in 2023 to become the latest addition to Enzo Maresca's squad.

A product of Everton's youth system, Cannon signed his first professional contract with the club in March 2021 and made his senior Toffees debut in a Carabao Cup clash at Bournemouth in November 2022. He made his Premier League bow during the same month, also against the Cherries, before moving on loan to Preston North End in January 2023. His spell at Deepdale was a fruitful one as he found the net eight times in 20 league appearances for Ryan Lowe's side.

Internationally, he has represented Republic of Ireland at youth level, and most recently earned a first call-up to the Under-21s team in March 2023, making his debut in a friendly against Iceland.

Yunus AKGÜN — 29

POSITION: Forward **COUNTRY:** Turkey **DOB:** 07/07/2000

The exciting winger joined the Foxes as Leicester City's seventh summer signing in August. A capped international with his native Turkey, the 23-year-old arrives from Süper Lig title holders Galatasaray, where he has spent the majority of his career after coming through the ranks at the Istanbul giants.

With additional UEFA Champions League experience on the attacker's CV, and five international caps to his name, including a debut against Faroe Islands in June 2022, Akgün will be hoping to hit the ground running as a Foxes player in Maresca's new-look side.

Mads HERMANSEN 30

POSITION: Goalkeeper   **COUNTRY:** Denmark   **DOB:** 11/07/2000

Growing up in the Danish city of Odense, Hermansen rose through the ranks to become the No.1 at his native side Brøndby IF, as well collecting caps for Denmark's youth international teams. Capturing the eyes, and hearts of the Danish fanbase, the young goalkeeper was awarded the Brøndby Player of the Year award for 2022.

Born this side of the millennium, Leicester's latest addition boasts over 80 appearances at a domestic, European and international stage. His competitive debut for the Club was a big one, with Hermansen making a crucial save during the opening-day Championship win over Coventry City at King Power Stadium.

Daniel IVERSEN — 31

POSITION: Goalkeeper **COUNTRY:** Denmark **DOB:** 19/07/1997

Gørding-born Denmark youth international Iversen joined City in 2018 and he has gained an impressive amount of Football League experience on loan with Preston North End in the Championship, Rotherham United in League 1 and Oldham Athletic in League 2.

Internationally, the talented goalkeeper has represented Denmark from Under-16s to Under-21s level and received his first call-up to the senior squad in 2019. After representing OH Leuven on loan in Belgium's top tier, Iversen's most successful loan spell was his second stint with Preston.

His Premier League debut for City arrived in March 2023 - starting a run of games for the Foxes in the top flight. Relegation would ultimately be confirmed at the end of the season, but Iversen impressed many with his performances.

Kasey McATEER — 35

POSITION: Midfielder **COUNTRY:** England **DOB:** 22/11/2001

Versatile midfielder Kasey McAteer recently made his league debut and scored his first goals for the Foxes after breaking through the Academy ranks. The highly rated 21-year-old, who has been with City's Academy since the age of eight, made his senior debut for the Foxes in a 4-0 Premier League win over Newcastle United in December 2021.

Now under Enzo Maresca's management, the Foxes started the 2023/24 season at home against Coventry City - with McAteer impressing in the Championship opener at right wing. Despite injury, he was back in the XI for a visit to Rotherham United later in the month and he scored both goals in a 2-1 win to send the Foxes top of the table.

EFL CHAMPIONSHIP SQUAD 2023/24

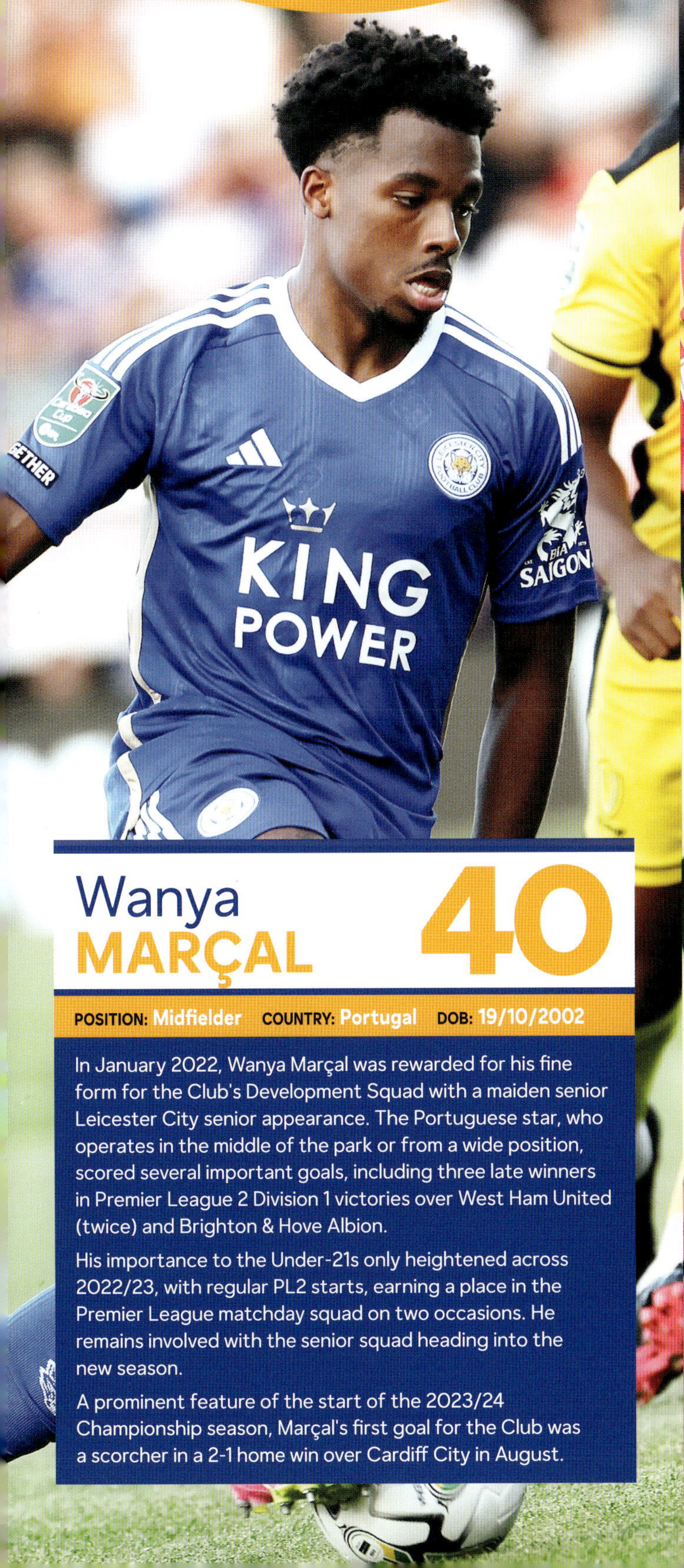

Wanya MARÇAL — 40

POSITION: Midfielder **COUNTRY:** Portugal **DOB:** 19/10/2002

In January 2022, Wanya Marçal was rewarded for his fine form for the Club's Development Squad with a maiden senior Leicester City senior appearance. The Portuguese star, who operates in the middle of the park or from a wide position, scored several important goals, including three late winners in Premier League 2 Division 1 victories over West Ham United (twice) and Brighton & Hove Albion.

His importance to the Under-21s only heightened across 2022/23, with regular PL2 starts, earning a place in the Premier League matchday squad on two occasions. He remains involved with the senior squad heading into the new season.

A prominent feature of the start of the 2023/24 Championship season, Marçal's first goal for the Club was a scorcher in a 2-1 home win over Cardiff City in August.

Jakub STOLARCZYK — 41

POSITION: Goalkeeper **COUNTRY:** Poland **DOB:** 19/12/2000

The Polish youth international goalkeeper, who joined the Foxes in 2019, has been a consistent and impressive performer for Leicester City's Under-21s. Stolarczyk earned professional experience with Dunfermline Athletic in Scotland's second tier during the 2021/22 season, conceding just 13 goals in 11 matches.

Stolarczyk made seven appearances in total out on loan to League 1 side Fleetwood, followed by 17 appearances for Hartlepool United during the 2022/23 season. He made his league debut for the Club in a victory against Huddersfield Town and kept a second successive clean sheet after starring in the Carabao Cup win at Burton Albion earlier that week too.

ONE OF THE HARDEST THINGS TO DO IN FOOTBALL IS TO STICK THE BALL IN THE BACK OF THE NET.

NOT LEAST BECAUSE THERE ARE USUALLY ELEVEN OTHER PLAYERS TRYING TO STOP YOU DOING JUST THAT!

SHOOTING FROM DISTANCE

Good service is obviously important, and a good understanding with your striking partner is also vital, but when it comes to spectacular strikes, practice is the key to hitting a consistently accurate and powerful shot and to developing the timing and power required.

EXERCISE

A small-sided pitch is set up with two 18-yard boxes put together, but the corners of the pitch are cut off as shown in the diagram. There are five players per team, including goalkeepers, but only one player is allowed in the opponent's half.

The aim of the drill is to work a shooting opportunity when you have the ball, with the likely chance being to shoot from outside your opponent's penalty area, from distance. The teams take it in turns to release the ball into play from their own 'keeper - usually by rolling out to an unmarked player.

18 YDS

KEY FACTORS

1. Attitude to shooting - be positive, have a go!
2. Technique - use laces, hit through the ball.
3. Do not sacrifice accuracy for power.
4. Wide angle shooting - aim for the far post.
5. Always follow up for rebounds!

The size of the pitch can be reduced for younger players, and it should be noted that these junior players should also be practicing with a size 4 or even a size 3 ball, depending on their age.

SOCCER SKILLS

LCFC WOMEN

Emile Heskey was appointed as the Club's new Head of Women's Football Development in October 2021, overseeing coaching, performance and recruitment at both senior and academy levels, bringing a wealth of experience to the role from a near 30-year career in the game.

Following the departure of Lydia Bedford and Assistant Manager Nicola Williams in November 2022, Willie Kirk became LCFC Women Manager, moving from his position as Director of Football - Women and Girls.

LCFC Women continued to play their home games at the Club's base, King Power Stadium, throughout the 2022/23 campaign. Demonstrating rapid progress and exponential growth, the Foxes are playing league fixtures in front of record crowds having more than doubled Season Ticket sales.

With a host of new signings joining the LCFC Women ranks in the summer, there is a strong sense of optimism about what lies ahead for the Foxes in 2023/24.

After 16 years of tireless efforts from a team of volunteers and part-time staff, rising up the divisions to the second tier of the women's game, collecting several trophies and honours along the way, the summer of 2020 saw LCFC Women officially become part of the Leicester City family.

It proved to be a historic season as promotion to the Women's Super League was secured for the very first time. Records were broken and milestones were met throughout the campaign as City embarked on a 12-game winning streak.

Moving into the Belvoir Drive training complex in January 2021, LCFC Women boast one of the most impressive women's-only facilities in English football, also housing the Club's Academy Pathway, which includes teams from age nine to 16-plus.

DAZZLING DEFENDERS

STEVE WALSH, MATT ELLIOTT AND WES MORGAN WERE THREE OF THE BEST DEFENDERS TO PULL ON THE BLUE SHIRT OF LEICESTER AND CONTINUING THAT TRADITION TODAY IS THE BELGIAN WOUT FAES.

Matt Elliott was a colossal presence at the heart of the Foxes' defence. Big players often come to the fore in big games and that was certainly the case for Elliott in the club's 1999/00 League Cup campaign.

A regular on Martin O'Neill's teamsheet in the Premier League, Elliott made six League Cup appearances in 1999/00 and weighed in with three vital goals. The powerful central defender scored the winning goal in the semi-final second leg against Aston Villa to propel the Foxes to Wembley and then produced a two-goal Man of the Match performance in the final as Tranmere Rovers were defeated 2-1.

Initially recruited from Oxford United in 1997 for a fee of £1.6M, Elliott became the cornerstone of the Foxes' defence for much of his Leicester City career.

Steve Walsh played 449 games for the Foxes over a 14-year period after signing from Wigan Athletic.

Walsh was a versatile player who also could play as a centre-forward. In his 449 games for Leicester he scored 62 goals. He was also club captain and led the Foxes to their famous 1995/96 Championship Play-Off final win over Crystal Palace and was also part of the squad that won the League Cup in 2000.

During his career he developed a reputation as one of the most uncompromising figures in football and was sent off 13 times - an EFL record.

STEVE WALSH

DATE OF BIRTH: 3 November, 1964
PLACE OF BIRTH: Fulwood
NATIONALITY: English
FOXES APPEARANCES: 449
FOXES GOALS: 62
FOXES DEBUT: 23 August, 1986
Leicester City 1-1 Luton Town (First Division)

MATT ELLIOTT

DATE OF BIRTH: 1 November, 1968
PLACE OF BIRTH: Wandsworth, London
NATIONALITY: Scottish
FOXES APPEARANCES: 290
FOXES GOALS: 33
FOXES DEBUT: 18 January, 1997
Leicester City 1-0 Wimbledon (Premier League)

Wes Morgan joined Leicester from his boyhood club Nottingham Forest and played for the Foxes until his retirement in 2021. In that time he captained them to their greatest triumph - the Premier League title of 2015/16.

Playing in central defence alongside Robert Huth, Morgan played every single minute of the Foxes' once-in-a-lifetime season, which saw them lose just three games on the way to their first-ever top-flight league title.

Morgan also made his mark on the international stage and played 30 times for Jamaica between 2013 and 2016, which included appearances in the 2015 CONCACAF Gold Cup final.

WES MORGAN

DATE OF BIRTH:	21 January, 1984
PLACE OF BIRTH:	Nottingham
NATIONALITY:	English, Jamaican
FOXES APPEARANCES:	323
FOXES GOALS:	14
FOXES DEBUT:	4 February, 2012

Brighton & Hove Albion 1-0 Leicester City (Championship)

WOUT FAES

DATE OF BIRTH:	3 April, 1998
PLACE OF BIRTH:	Mol, Belgium
NATIONALITY:	Belgian
FOXES APPEARANCES:	40*
FOXES GOALS:	1*
FOXES DEBUT:	17 September, 2022

Tottenham Hotspur 6-2 Leicester City (Premier League)

*CORRECT AS OF AUGUST 2023

Wout Faes arrived in Leicester on 1 September 2022 from Reims and despite making his debut in a 6-2 defeat at Tottenham he won praise for the immediate impact he had on a struggling Foxes' defence.

Although Leicester City were relegated in 2022/23, Faes continued to be one of the few players to impress in a team that came up short in its battle for survival.

He did however suffer the ignominy of being only the fourth Premier League player ever to score two own goals in a game in their 2-1 defeat at Liverpool. He was also part of Belgium's 2022 World Cup squad.

FOOTY PHRASES

ALL OF THESE FOOTY PHRASES ARE HIDDEN IN THE GRID, EXCEPT FOR ONE ...BUT CAN YOU WORK OUT WHICH ONE?
ANSWERS ON PAGE 62

```
C A E S W Y V V B H U G N U R Y M M U D
V U Q I D E R B Y D A Y O L U R T S S U
K F A D J L G T X T F C B E I A K C F P
I B H E O T L P Z R V N M W O J I R Y A
C M O F F S I D E R U L E E D S P E Y H
M E R U E I J R D E D A Q G S H L A X C
R X E R N H A T T R I C K O I L A M R T
E I Y O W W S L S N O W R S O Z Y E Y A
D C A A Z L W S J K T K Y V K B M R T M
A A L P X A U Y H M I D F I E D A R O E
E N P T K N F W G C P L J K A M K N L H
H W E J A I L O K H A O F O H I E C G T
G A M E O F T W O H A L V E S T R N U F
N V A I A H E S L F J D U A O I U O T O
I E G B I C L A S S A C T U P F G E V N
V D G O A E E U C K S S C Y W U L Q L A
I R I R Q G M N S A C H G H D O S F G M
D V B A C K O F T H E N E T Z P X B N A
```

Back of the Net	Diving Header	Half Volley	Offside Rule
Big Game Player	Dugout	Hat-trick	One-touch
Brace	Dummy Run	Keepie Uppie	Playmaker
Class Act	Final Whistle	Man of the Match	Scissor Kick
Derby Day	Game of Two Halves	Mexican Wave	Screamer

29

PLAYERS OF THE SEASON

Nigeria international Kelechi Iheanacho won the Men's first-team POTS prize after netting 13 goals in all competitions for the Foxes over the course of the 2022/23 campaign.

With a habit of hitting form in-front of goal at crucial moments, with his 2021 FA Cup heroics serving as a suitable reminder of just that, the talented striker's performances in an otherwise disappointing season reminded supporters once more why he has cemented himself as a fans' favourite over the years.

Despite being named in the starting line-up on only thirteen occasions, Iheanacho strikes helped City to wins over Aston Villa and Tottenham in February, when he scored twice and assisted three more goals across both games. The former Manchester City star produced a moment to remember in a 1-1 draw against Leeds United, assisting Jamie Vardy for his equaliser, despite being injured.

Iheanacho joins an impressive list of previous Men's first-team POTS award winners, which includes the likes of James Maddison, Youri Tielemans and Jamie Vardy in the past three years alone.

Germany youth international Janina Leitzig collected both the Women's Player of the Season and the Women's Players' Player of the Season awards.

Despite only joining LCFC Women in January, on loan from Bayern Munich, Leitzig has made a superb impact for Willie Kirk's side, who sealed survival in the Barclays Women's Super League. Over 13 outings, the German stopper helped City's Women overturn a seven-point deficit at the base of the WSL table and finish the season in 10th - their highest-ever finish.

At Academy level, winger Tawanda Maswanhise was chosen as the Club's Men's Development Squad Player of the Season.

The talented forward struck seven goals in Premier League 2 Division 1 last term. Youngster Denny Draper was also named Women's Academy Player of the Season after helping the Club's Women's Academy Team to finish seventh in the FA WSL Academy League.

JANINA LEITZIG

TOP CLASS PLAYERS NOT ONLY NEED TO WIN THE BALL IN MIDFIELD, BUT ALSO PROVIDE THAT CUTTING EDGE WHEN NEEDED TO BE ABLE TO PLAY THROUGH DEFENCES WITH QUICK, INCISIVE PASSING.

THE WALL PASS

With teams being very organised in modern football, it can be very difficult to break them down and create scoring opportunities. One of the best ways to achieve this is by using the 'wall pass', otherwise known as the quick one-two.

EXERCISE

In a non-pressurised situation, involving four players, A carries the ball forward towards a static defender (in this case a cone) and before reaching the defender, plays the ball to B before running around the opposite side to receive the one-touch return pass. A then delivers the ball safely to C who then repeats the exercise returning the ball to D, and in this way the exercise continues. Eventually a defender can be used to make the exercise more challenging, with all players being rotated every few minutes.

The exercise can progress into a five-a-side game, the diagram below shows how additional players (W) on the touchline can be used as 'walls' with just one touch available to help the man in possession of the ball.

Each touchline player can move up and down the touchline, but not enter the pitch - they can also play for either team.

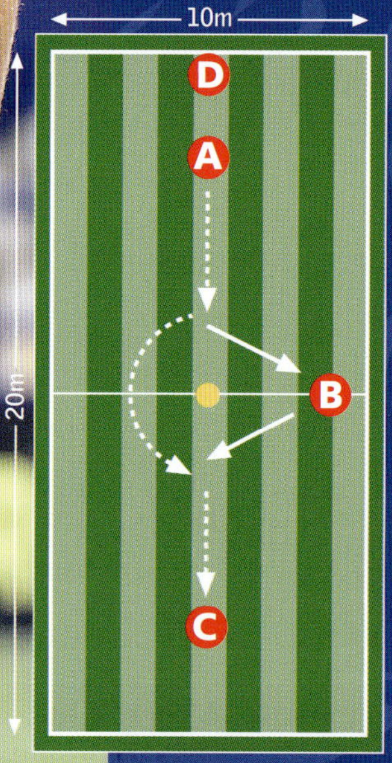

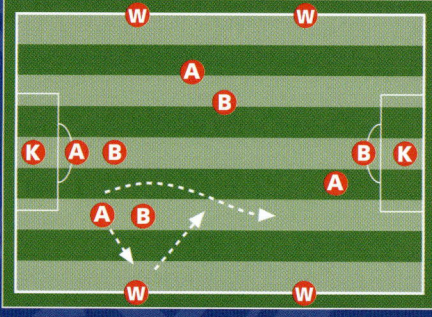

KEY FACTORS

1. Look to commit the defender before passing - do not play the ball too early.
2. Pass the ball firmly and to feet.
3. Accelerate past defender after passing.
4. Receiver (B) make themselves available for the pass.
5. B delivers a return pass, weighted correctly, into space.

If done correctly, this is a tactic which is extremely difficult to stop, but needs teamwork and communication between the two attacking players.

SOCCER SKILLS

A-Z

ARE YOU READY TO TACKLE OUR A-Z FOOTBALL QUIZ?

THE SIMPLE RULE IS THAT THE ANSWERS RUN THROUGH THE 26 LETTERS OF THE ALPHABET.

A What nationality is Watford goalkeeper Daniel Bachmann?

A

B Which team won the Championship title in 2022/23?

B

C Which Premier League club reappointed their former manager as interim in March 2023?

C

D Which League 1 side play their home matches at Pride Park?

D

E What nationality is Liverpool's sensational striker Mohamed Salah?

E

F Which country knocked England out of the FIFA World Cup finals in 2022?

F

G Which famous football ground, pictured above, is due to host its final fixture in 2024?

G _____

H Which club did Neil Warnock lead to Championship survival in 2022/23?

H _____

I Which country did England defeat 6-2 in their opening game of the FIFA 2022 World Cup finals?

I _____

J Aston Villa winger Leon Bailey plays internationally for which country?

J _____

K What is the name of Premier League new boys Luton Town's home ground?

K _____

L Can you name the Ipswich Town striker who netted 17 League 1 goals in the Tractor Boys' 2022/23 promotion-winning season?

L _____

M Which Championship club boasted the division's top scorer in 2022/23?

M _____

ANSWERS ON PAGE 62

Q Can you name the country that hosted the FIFA 2022 World Cup finals?

Q

R Which Spanish side did Manchester City defeat in last season's UEFA Champions League semi-final?

R

S Which team knocked Premier League champions Manchester City out of the Carabao Cup last season?

S

N

What nationality is Manchester City's ace marksman Erling Haaland?

N

O Can you name the former Premier League team that will compete in the National League in 2023/24?

O

T Which full-back left Huddersfield Town to join Nottingham Forest ahead of their return to the Premier League in the summer of 2022?

T

P Which international striker ended five seasons with Norwich City in May 2023?

P

U Can you name Brighton's German forward who joined the Seagulls in January 2022?

U

V Can you name the former England striker who has hit over 100 Premier League goals for Leicester City?

V

W Can you name the goalkeeper who got his name on the scoresheet last season in a Championship fixture?

W

X Can you name the Portuguese international defender who played in the Premier League with Everton, Liverpool & Middlesbrough?

X

Y At which club did Leeds United's Luke Ayling make his league debut?

Y

Z Which Dutch international midfielder played Premier League football for Chelsea, Middlesbrough and Liverpool in the 2000s?

Z

A-Z
PART TWO

ANSWERS ON PAGE 62

DESIGN A FOOTY BOOT

Design a brilliant new footy boot for the Foxes squad!

MIDFIELD MAESTROS

MUZZY IZZET, ANDY KING AND N'GOLO KANTE HAVE ALL PLAYED LEADING ROLES IN THE HEART OF THE LEICESTER MIDFIELD, WITH KIERNAN DEWSBURY-HALL PULLING THOSE SAME STRINGS IN THE CURRENT LEICESTER TEAM.

Muzzy Izzet officially signed for the Foxes from Chelsea in the summer of 1996, but had already spent the final two months of the 1995/96 season at Filbert Street on loan. His energetic style quickly made him a favourite with the Leicester faithful.

Alongside Neil Lennon, he played a key role in the engine room of the Leicester side that punched above its weight in the mid-to-late 1990s and which went on to win two League Cups.

In addition to a stellar domestic career, Izzet also played international football for Turkey, winning nine caps and playing in the 2002 World Cup.

Andy King completed a hat-trick of title triumphs as a Leicester City player having won League 1 (2008/09), the Championship (2013/14) and the Premier League (2015/16) during a sensational career at the King Power Stadium.

An exciting all-action midfielder, King progressed through the youth ranks to make his first-team debut in 2007. His commitment to the blue shirt and club crest made him an extremely popular player with supporters and team-mates alike. He was voted the Club's Young Player of the Year in 2008/09 and Players' Player of the Year in both 2009/10 and 2010/11.

A full Wales international, King also represented the Foxes in their 2016/17 UEFA Champions League campaign.

MUZZY IZZET

DATE OF BIRTH: 31 October, 1974
PLACE OF BIRTH: London
NATIONALITY: English, Turkish
FOXES APPEARANCES: 269
FOXES GOALS: 38
FOXES DEBUT: 30 March, 1996
Leicester City 0-2 Sheffield United (Division One)

ANDY KING

DATE OF BIRTH: 29 October, 1988
PLACE OF BIRTH: Barnstaple
NATIONALITY: Welsh
FOXES APPEARANCES: 379
FOXES GOALS: 62
FOXES DEBUT: 2 October, 2007
Leicester City 0-0 Wolves (Championship)

N'Golo Kante joined Leicester from Caen in August 2015 as a replacement for the departed Esteban Cambiasso. He went on to exceed all expectations and play a central role in the Foxes' Premier League title triumph.

His stay at Leicester was relatively short - one season and 40 games - but in that time he earned himself legendary status among Leicester fans for his outstanding performances. In his role as a defensive midfielder, he made a record 175 tackles and 157 interceptions.

He left Leicester City in the summer of 2016 for Chelsea and now plays in the Saudi Pro League for Al-Ittihad.

N'GOLO KANTE

DATE OF BIRTH: 29 March, 1991
PLACE OF BIRTH: Paris, France
NATIONALITY: French
FOXES APPEARANCES: 40
FOXES GOALS: 1
FOXES DEBUT: 8 August, 2015
Leicester City 4-2 Sunderland (Premier League)

KIERNAN DEWSBURY-HALL

DATE OF BIRTH: 6 September, 1998
PLACE OF BIRTH: Nottingham
NATIONALITY: English
FOXES APPEARANCES: 84*
FOXES GOALS: 7*
FOXES DEBUT: 25 January, 2020
Brentford 0-1 Leicester City (FA Cup)

*CORRECT AS OF AUGUST 2023

Kiernan Dewsbury-Hall is a product of the Leicester City Academy, which he joined as an eight-year-old in 2006. In order to gain experience he was loaned to Blackpool and Luton, but not before signing his first pro contract for the Foxes in 2017.

During the loan spell at Luton in 2020/21 he made his big breakthrough, ending that season with the Hatters' Player of the Season award. He returned to Leicester for the 2021/22 season and has not looked back since.

For 2023/24, he will be a senior figure in Leicester's midfield as they look to bounce back to the Premier League.

CLASSIC FAN'TASTIC

Filbert the Fox is hiding in the Wembley crowd in five different places as City fans enjoy the Community Shield atmosphere in 2016. **Can you find all five?** ANSWERS ON PAGE 62

43

2 JAMES JUSTIN

5 CALLUM DOYLE

GOALS
OF THE SEASON

With only a minute of the first 45 to go, Justin cut in from the right wing, playing a give-and-go with Dennis Praet, and bent a beautiful left-footed shot into the inside of the post from 20 yards to put the Foxes deservedly in front

FOXES 2-2 BRENTFORD
PREMIER LEAGUE · 7 AUGUST, 2022

Just 30 seconds into the second period, City doubled their advantage through a Kiernan Dewsbury-Hall stunner. Jamie Vardy touched the ball into the No.22's path, and he did the rest, slamming a daisy-cutter in off the foot of David Raya's left-hand post.

'You're my Dewsbury-Hall' bellowed around King Power Stadium. City were deservedly two goals to the good through Timothy Castagne's header and a special strike from Kiernan Dewsbury-Hall, but Ivan Toney pulled one back before Josh Dasilva scored a stylish equaliser to ensure the spoils were shared.

YOURI TIELEMANS
WOLVES 0-4 FOXES
PREMIER LEAGUE · 23 OCTOBER, 2022

City weathered the early storm at Molineux and Youri Tielemans' thumping effort on eight minutes set the visitors on their way to a first away win of the season.

The Foxes took the lead in emphatic fashion. Harvey Barnes was brought down by Jonny - carded for his troubles - on the left flank and James Maddison was the man to whip in the free-kick. It was initially headed away, but only to the feet of Tielemans, who unleashed a fearsome half-volley into the top left corner to add to his catalogue of wonderstrikes.

JAMES JUSTIN
FOXES 3-0 NEWPORT COUNTY
LEAGUE CUP · 8 NOVEMBER, 2022

While the Welsh outfit had remained compact throughout large parts of the first half, when James Justin burst into space on the edge of the box, Nick Townsend could do nothing about his strike as he curled in from distance in brilliant fashion.

KIERNAN
DEWSBURY-HALL

BEHIND THE BADGE

CAN YOU IDENTIFY EVERY ONE OF THESE FOXES STARS...

...HIDDEN BEHIND OUR BEAUTIFUL BADGE?

A

B

C

D

E

F

G

H

49

HARRY
WINKS
8

TRUE COLOURS

HAVE FUN COLOURING IN THIS PICTURE OF FOXES STAR HARRY WINKS

FORMIDABLE FORWARDS

GARY LINEKER, EMILE HESKEY AND RIYAD MAHREZ WERE ALL TOP FOXES MARKSMEN, AND CURRENTLY LEADING THEIR LINE IS ANOTHER CLUB LEGEND, JAMIE VARDY.

Gary Lineker was a Leicester City goalscoring legend in the 1980s, but you probably know him as presenter of BBC's Match of the Day. Born and raised in Leicester, Lineker joined his hometown club from school and went on to score over 100 City goals.

After leaving Leicester, Lineker played for Everton, Barcelona, Tottenham and Grampus Eight (Japan), but his seven-year stay at Filbert Street was his longest and Leicester City is the club that remains the closest to his heart.

In his 80 games for England he scored 48 goals, including England's goal in the 1990 World Cup semi-final against West Germany.

GARY LINEKER

DATE OF BIRTH: 30 November, 1960
PLACE OF BIRTH: Leicester
NATIONALITY: English
FOXES APPEARANCES: 216
FOXES GOALS: 103
FOXES DEBUT: 1 January, 1979
Leicester City 2-0 Oldham Athletic (Division Two)

Emile Heskey was also born and bred in Leicester and joined the Club's Academy aged just nine. He signed his first pro contract eight years later and enjoyed an exceptional six seasons with the Foxes, scoring 46 goals in nearly 200 appearances.

He was part of the successful Leicester team that won the League Cup in 1997 and 2000, and in the summer of 2000 made an £11M move to Liverpool.

A strong, powerful and mobile striker, Heskey also led the line for England 62 times and famously scored in England's 5-1 win over Germany in Munich in 2001.

EMILE HESKEY

DATE OF BIRTH: 11 January, 1978
PLACE OF BIRTH: Leicester
NATIONALITY: English
FOXES APPEARANCES: 197
FOXES GOALS: 48
FOXES DEBUT: 16 August, 2014
Leicester City 2-0 Middlesbrough (Premier League)

Riyad Mahrez joined Leicester from Le Havre in 2014 and was part of the famous Class of 2016 that won the Premier League against all the odds. He spent five highly successful seasons at the King Power before signing for Manchester City in a £60m move.

Despite his slender build, Mahrez's outstanding technique, silky skills and lovely left foot have made him one of the best wingers in world football, and those five years at Leicester City formed a key part of his development.

He has also made over 80 appearances for Algeria and was named African Footballer of the Year in 2016.

RIYAD MAHREZ

DATE OF BIRTH: 21 February, 1991
PLACE OF BIRTH: Sarcelles, France
NATIONALITY: Algerian
FOXES APPEARANCES: 179
FOXES GOALS: 48
FOXES DEBUT: 16 August, 2014
Leicester City 2-0 Middlesbrough (Premier League)

JAMIE VARDY

DATE OF BIRTH: 11 January, 1987
PLACE OF BIRTH: Sheffield
NATIONALITY: English
FOXES APPEARANCES: 430*
FOXES GOALS: 170*
FOXES DEBUT: 17 August, 2012
Torquay United 0-4 Leicester City (League Cup)

*CORRECT AS OF AUGUST 2023

Jamie Vardy signed for Leicester in 2012 from then-Conference team Fleetwood Town. Prior to joining the Foxes he had only played in non-league football and so was keen to make up for lost time, which he did by scoring lots of goals!

Vardy is now in his 12th season with Leicester City and is currently third in their list of all-time leading goalscorers. He was a key member of the 2015/16 Premier League title-winning team, scoring 24 goals.

A hard-working striker who can use both feet effectively, he has also represented England - winning 26 caps and scoring seven goals.

REWIND

THREE GREAT FOXES VICTORIES FROM 2023

Leicester City 4
Tottenham Hotspur 1

PREMIER LEAGUE • 11 FEBRUARY, 2023

A sensational first-half display from Leicester City set the team on their way to back-to-back Premier League victories as they defeated Tottenham Hotspur 4-1 in February.

Having beaten Aston Villa 4-2 away a week earlier, Leicester did not let the disappointment of conceding a 14th-minute opener to Spurs' Rodrigo Bentancur set them back. Roared on by a passionate King Power crowd, the Foxes scored twice in two minutes through Nampalys Mendy and James Maddison to turn the match around. The home side then returned to the dressing room 3-1 up at the break thanks to Kelechi Iheanacho's goal deep into first-half injury time.

Harvey Barnes added the fourth nine minutes from time as the team showed that on their day they really were a match for anyone.

Leicester City 2
Wolverhampton Wanderers 1

PREMIER LEAGUE • 22 APRIL, 2023

The Foxes produced an impressive performance to defeat Wolverhampton Wanderers 2-1 at King Power Stadium in April - a result that boosted the team's Premier League survival chances.

Under the management of Dean Smith at King Power for the first time, the Foxes bounced back from falling a goal behind to take all three points. The comeback began with Kelechi Iheanacho's first-half equaliser from the penalty spot.

Timothy Castagne then bagged the Foxes' all-important winner 15 minutes from time to inject a major dose of belief into the Club as the team ended a ten-match winless streak in style.

Leicester City 2
Coventry City 1

CHAMPIONSHIP • AUGUST 6, 2023

Enzo Maresca's Leicester City spell began with a dramatic 2-1 comeback victory over M69 foes Coventry City to kick-start the Foxes' EFL Championship promotion bid.

A brace from Kiernan Dewsbury-Hall over a late 10-minute spell overturned Kyle McFadzean's opener at the climax of a pulsating derby-day encounter.

On 76 minutes, City levelled and King Power Stadium burst in relief, but the Foxes faithful wanted more. In a flash, Filbert Way was bouncing. Leicester were now in front. Patient play eventually led to Madividi holding it in the box. He fed Dewsbury-Hall and the Academy graduate launched it past Wilson and into the top corner.

FAST FORWARD

...AND THREE BIG EFL CHAMPIONSHIP ENCOUNTERS TO COME IN 2024...

Leeds United (AWAY)

CHAMPIONSHIP · 24 FEBRUARY, 2024

Just like the Foxes, Leeds United suffered relegation from the Premier League last season and will be strongly fancied to mount a serious bid for promotion back to the top flight at the first time of asking.

The Elland Road club are now under the management of former Norwich City head coach Daniel Farke. The German won the Championship title twice with the Canaries and will be going in search of a hat-trick of second tier titles in 2023/24.

Leeds will provide our fifth and final Championship opponents in the busy month of February and the match at Elland Road on February 24 certainly appears one not to miss.

Southampton (HOME)

CHAMPIONSHIP · 16 MARCH, 2024

Southampton complete the trio of teams relegated from the Premier League in 2022/23 and are sure to provide a tough challenge here at King Power Stadium when they take on Enzo Maresca's men in mid-March.

The Saints are another club that made a managerial change in the summer of 2023 with former MK Dons and Swansea City head coach Russell Martin being the man appointed to spearhead their promotion ambitions for 2023/24.

Early season form indicated that the Saints could well be the division's great entertainers after an opening night 2-1 victory at Sheffield Wednesday, but they were brought back to earth when the Foxes visited St Mary's in September and went home with three points and a 4-1 victory.

West Bromwich Albion (HOME)

CHAMPIONSHIP · 20 APRIL, 2024

The Foxes' penultimate home match of the season sees a Midlands derby take place with Carlos Corberán's WBA coming to King Power Stadium on April 20.

Although Albion are now in their third season outside of the Premier League, the Baggies still have a number of quality players at their disposal and are sure to make life difficult for the Foxes - particularly with both Midlands pride at stake.

Albion ended last season in ninth place and three points shy of the Play-Off places, suffice to say they will be searching for better times in 2024 and this April's meeting between the two sides at the business end of the season could well prove vital.

BEING PREDICTABLE IS EASY IN FOOTBALL.

DOING THE UNEXPECTED IS A LOT MORE DIFFICULT.

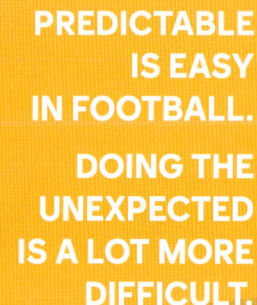

TURNING WITH THE BALL

One of the biggest problems a defence can have to deal with is when a skilful player is prepared to turn with the ball and run at them, committing a key defender into making a challenge. Because football today is so fast and space so precious, this is becoming a rare skill.

EXERCISE 1

In an area 20m x 10m, A plays the ball into B who turns, and with two touches maximum plays the ball into C. C controls and reverses the process. After a few minutes the middleman is changed.

As you progress, a defender is brought in to oppose B, and is initially encouraged to play a 'passive' role. B has to turn and play the ball to C who is allowed to move along the baseline.

The type of turns can vary. Players should be encouraged to use the outside of the foot, inside of the foot, with feint and disguise to make space for the turn.

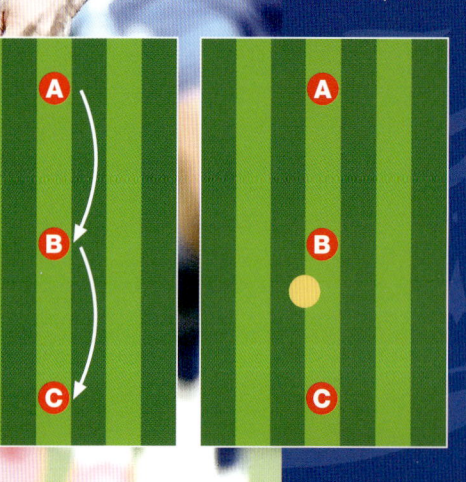

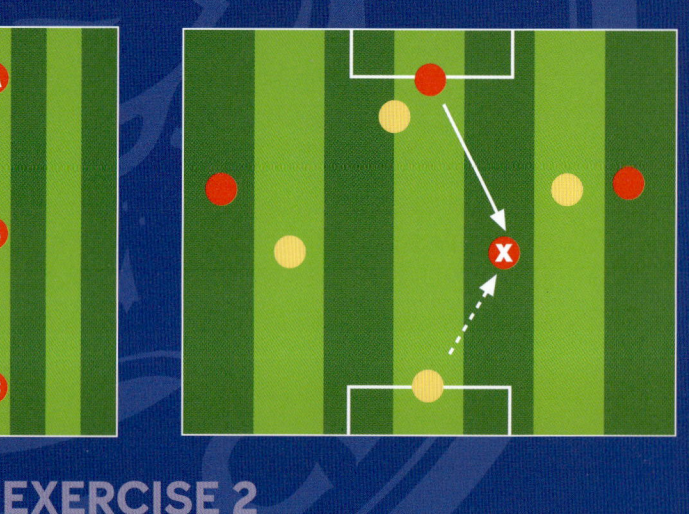

EXERCISE 2

As the players grow in confidence, you can move forward to a small-sided game. In this example of a 4-a-side practice match, X has made space for himself to turn with the ball, by coming off his defender at an angle. By doing this he can see that the defender has not tracked him, and therefore has the awareness to turn and attack.

Matches at the top level are won and lost by pieces of skill such as this, so players have to be brave enough to go in search of the ball, and turn in tight situations.

SOCCER SKILLS

10 STEPHY MAVIDIDI

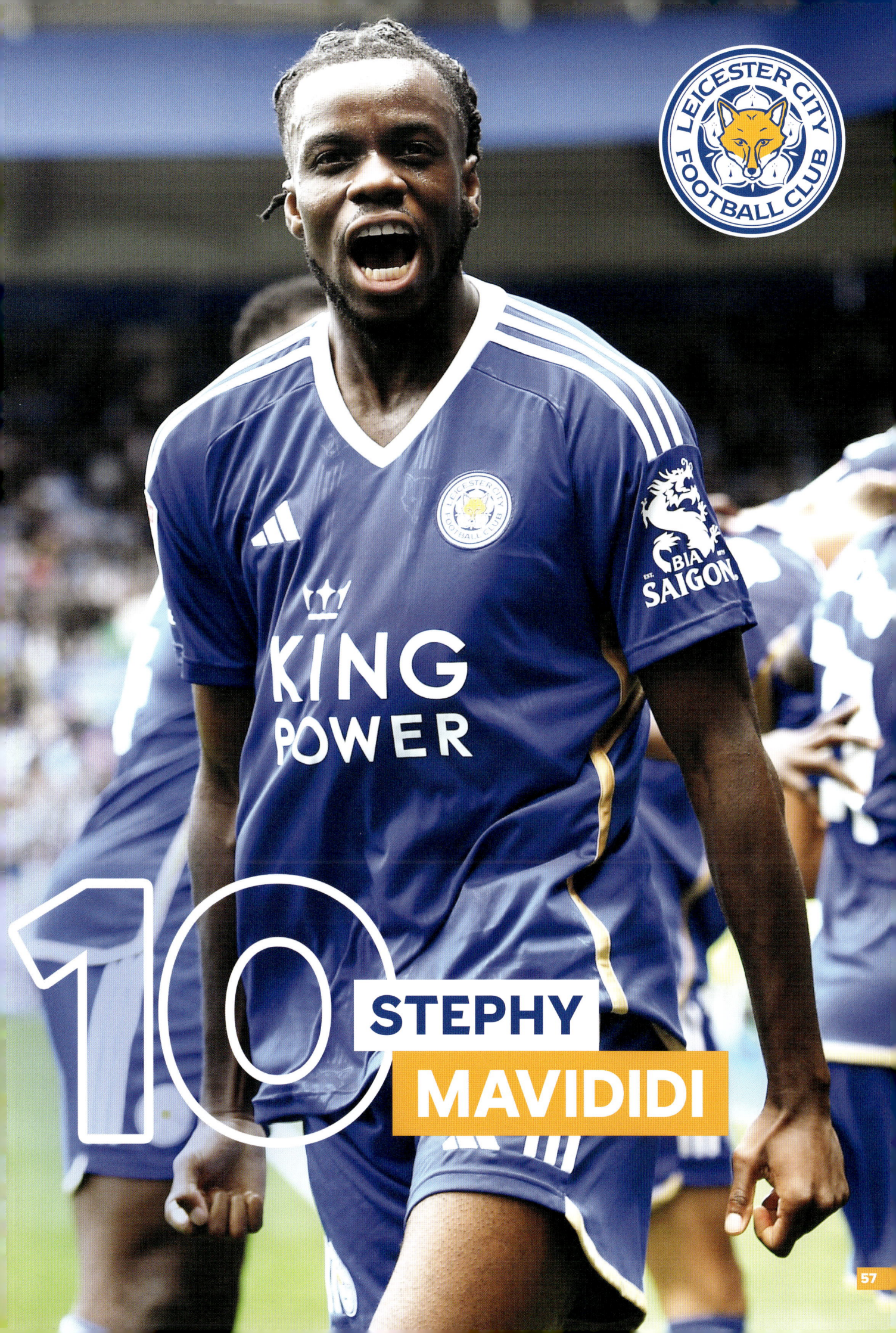

HIGH FIVES

TEST YOUR LEICESTER CITY KNOWLEDGE & MEMORY WITH OUR HIGH FIVES QUIZ

1. Across the previous five seasons, who have been Leicester City's leading league goalscorers?

1. _____
2. _____
3. _____
4. _____
5. _____

2. Can you name the Foxes' last five FA Cup opponents ahead of the 2023/24 season?

1. _____
2. _____
3. _____
4. _____
5. _____

3. Prior to Enzo Maresca, who were the Club's last five permanent managers?

1. _____
2. _____
3. _____
4. _____
5. _____

4. Can you name our last five EFL Cup opponents as at the end of the 2022/23 season?

1. _____
2. _____
3. _____
4. _____
5. _____

5. Can you name the trophies that Leicester City won in the following seasons?

1. 2020/21
2. 2015/16
3. 2013/14
4. 2008/09
5. 1999/00

6. Which members of the Leicester City squad started the most league fixtures last season?

1.
2.
3.
4.
5.

7. Can you recall the following players' squad numbers from the 2022/23 season?

1. James Justin
2. Marc Albrighton
3. Kelechi Iheanacho
4. Patson Daka
5. Dennis Praet

8. Can you recall the scoreline and season from our last five victories over rivals Nottingham Forest?

1.
2.
3.
4.
5.

9. Can you remember the Foxes' final five Premier League victories from last season?

1.
2.
3.
4.
5.

1. Can you recall the Club's end of season points tally from the last five seasons?

1.
2.
3.
4.
5.

ANSWERS ON PAGE 62

SENSATIONAL STOPPERS

PETER SHILTON, KASEY KELLER AND KASPER SCHMEICHEL ARE ALL FOXES GOALKEEPING LEGENDS. CITY'S CURRENT MAINSTAY BETWEEN THE STICKS IS MADS HERMANSEN.

Peter Shilton is regarded as one of the best goalkeepers both in Leicester City and English history. He was a superb shot-stopper and had fine aerial ability. He also had a great sense of positioning and was always in command of his area.

Shilton made his first-team debut as a 16-year-old, covering for Gordon Banks, who played for England that night. Since taking over from Banksy, Shilts rarely missed a game for City and during his time with the Foxes, he scored the only goal of his career at Southampton in 1967, played in the 1969 FA Cup final against Manchester City, gained promoted again in 1971, and won the Charity (Community) Shield by beating Liverpool three months later.

The legendary goalkeeper also won the first 20 of his record-total of 125 England caps while at Filbert Street. Shilton went on to play at three World Cups for England, conceding only 10 goals in 17 games.

PETER SHILTON

DATE OF BIRTH: 18 September, 1949
PLACE OF BIRTH: Leicester
NATIONALITY: English
FOXES APPEARANCES: 339
FOXES DEBUT: 4 May, 1966
Leicester City 3-0 Everton (First Division)

Kasey Keller arrived at Leicester in the summer of 1996 and in his first season played a vital role in the Foxes winning the League Cup.

Signed from Millwall, the USA international 'keeper arrived in the East Midlands in August 1996 after four successful seasons with the South London club. He spent three Premier League seasons with the Foxes, which also include a brief run in the 1997/98 UEFA and another League Cup final in 1999.

Keller was at Leicester for a period of unexpected success for the Club and was known for his excellent shot-stopping and command of his penalty box.

KASEY KELLER

DATE OF BIRTH: 29 November, 1969
PLACE OF BIRTH: Washington DC, USA
NATIONALITY: American
FOXES APPEARANCES: 99
FOXES DEBUT: 17 August, 1996
Sunderland 0-0 Leicester City (Premier League)

Kasper Schmeichel joined the Foxes from Leeds United in June 2011, but started his career at Manchester City before making a surprise move to Notts County.

The son of legendary Manchester United 'keeper Peter Schmeichel, Kasper spent 11 successful seasons at King Power Stadium, which included the never-to-be-forgotten Premier League title triumph in 2015/16.

Schmeichel was known for his commanding presence in his penalty box and excellent shot-stopping. He has been a regular in the Danish national team since 2013 and has won over 90 caps for his country.

KASPER SCHMEICHEL

DATE OF BIRTH:	5 November, 1986
PLACE OF BIRTH:	Copenhagen, Denmark
NATIONALITY:	Danish
FOXES APPEARANCES:	479
FOXES DEBUT:	6 August, 2011

Coventry City 0-1 Leicester City (Premier League)

MADS HERMANSEN

DATE OF BIRTH:	11 July, 2000
PLACE OF BIRTH:	Odense, Denmark
NATIONALITY:	Danish
FOXES APPEARANCES:	2*
FOXES:	6 August, 2023

Leicester City 2-1 Coventry City (Championship)

*CORRECT AS OF AUGUST 2023

Mads Hermansen signed for Leicester in the summer of 2023 from Brøndby of Denmark on a five-year deal and is looking to establish himself at the Foxes' number one.

Leicester will be hoping Hermansen enjoys the same level of success at King Power as his compatriot Schmeichel and the early signs are promising.

The 23-year-old has also played for Denmark at U16 to U21 levels and was called up to the senior squad for the Euro 2024 qualifiers. Hermansen is known for his ability to competently play the 'sweeper-keeper' role and in Denmark is considered a penalty-saving specialist.

ANSWERS

PAGE 29: FOOTY PHRASES
Keepie Uppie.

PAGE 34: A-Z QUIZ
A. Austrian. B. Burnley. C. Crystal Palace. D. Derby County. E. Egyptian. F. France. G. Goodison Park (Everton). H. Huddersfield Town. I. Iran. J. Jamaica. K. Kenilworth Road. L. Ladapo, Freddie. M. Middlesbrough (Chuba Akpom). N. Norwegian. O. Oldham Athletic. P. Pukki, Teemu. Q. Qatar. R. Real Madrid. S. Southampton. T. Toffolo, Harry. U. Undav, Deniz. V. Vardy, Jamie. W. Wilson, Ben (Coventry City). X. Xavier, Abel. Y. Yeovil Town. Z. Zenden, Boudewijn.

PAGE 42: FAN'TASTIC

PAGE 48: BEHIND THE BADGE
A. Stephy Mavididi. B. Wilfred Ndidi. C. Ricardo Pereira. D. Marc Albrighton. E. Cesare Casadei. F. Wout Faes. G. Jamie Vardy. H. Kelechi Iheanacho.

PAGE 58: HIGH FIVES

QUIZ 1:
1. 2022/23, Harvey Barnes (13 goals).
2. 2021/22, Jamie Vardy (15 goals).
3. 2020/21, Jamie Vardy (15 goals).
4. 2019/20, Jamie Vardy (23 goals).
5. 2018/19, Jamie Vardy (18 goals).

QUIZ 2:
1. 2022/23, Blackburn Rovers (fifth round).
2. 2022/23, Walsall (fourth round).
3. 2022/23, Gillingham (third round).
4. 2021/22, Watford (third round).
5. 2021/22, Nottingham Forest (fourth round).

QUIZ 3:
1. Dean Smith. 2. Brendan Rodgers. 3. Claude Puel. 4. Craig Shakespeare. 5. Claudio Ranieri.

QUIZ 4:
1. Newcastle United (2022/23). 2. MK Dons (2022/23).
3. Newport County (2022/23). 4. Stockport County (2022/23)
5. Liverpool (2021/22).

QUIZ 5:
1. 2020/21, FA Cup winners. 2. 2015/16, Premier League Champions.
3. 2013/14, EFL Championship winners. 4. 2008/09, League One Champions.
5. 1999/00, League Cup winners.

QUIZ 6:
1. Timothy Castagne (36 Premier League starts).
2. Harvey Barnes (32 Premier League starts).
3. Wout Faes (31 Premier League starts).
4. James Maddison & Kieran Dewsbury-Hall (28 Premier League starts).
5. Youri Tielemans (27 Premier League starts).

QUIZ 7:
1. 2. 2. 11. 3. 14. 4. 20. 5. 26.

QUIZ 8:
1. 2022/23, Leicester City 4 Nottingham Forest 0 (Premier League).
2. 2012/13, Nottingham Forest 2 Leicester City 3 (Championship).
3. 2011/12, Leicester City 4 Nottingham Forest 0 (FA Cup).
4. 2010/11, Leicester City 1 Nottingham Forest 0 (Championship).
5. 2009/10, Leicester City 3 Nottingham Forest 0 (Championship).

QUIZ 9:
1. Leicester City 2 West Ham United 1.
2. Leicester City 2 Wolverhampton Wanderers 1.
3. Leicester City 2 Tottenham Hotspur 1.
4. Aston Villa 2 Leicester City 4.
5. West Ham United 0 Leicester City 2.

QUIZ 10:
1. 2022/23, 34 points. 2. 2021/22, 52 points. 3. 2020/21, 66 points.
4. 2019/20, 62 points. 5. 2018/19, 52 points.